PAINTING
CERAMICS

PAINTING CERAMICS

CAROLINE GREEN

NEW HOLLAND

This edition published in 2003 by
New Holland Publishers (UK) Ltd
London · Cape Town · Sydney · Auckland

Garfield House, 86-88 Edgware Road
London W2 2EA
United Kingdom
www.newhollandpublishers.com

80 McKenzie Street
Cape Town 8001
South Africa

Level 1, Unit 4, 14 Aquatic Drive
Frenchs Forest, NSW 2086
Australia

218 Lake Road
Northcote, Auckland
New Zealand

ISBN 1 85974 288 2

Editor: Alice Bell
Photographer: John Freeman
Assistant Editor: Anke Ueberberg

Editorial Direction: Rosemary Wilkinson

10 9 8 7 6 5 4 3 2 1

Reproduced by
PICA Colour Separation, Singapore
Printed and bound in Malaysia by
Times Offset (M) Sdn. Bhd.

Acknowledgements

Many thanks to John Wright of Pébéo UK for
the generous provision of different paints,
pens and outliners that have been used
extensively in this book and to Carol Hook of
Clear Communications Ltd for all her help
and information on the products provided.

Also thanks to Paul Shute of F. Trauffler Ltd
whose generous supply of Apilco white
porcelain has made the most of my designs.

Also grateful thanks to Judy Balchin and
Duncan Green for allowing me to show some
of their china painting in the gallery sections
of the book.

Contents

Introduction

People have been painting ceramics and chinaware for centuries, both for use in the home and as beautiful items to display. Taking influences from the past and present and using some of the latest ceramic paint products, you too can produce your own stunning designs.

You do not have to be an expert artist to paint ceramics, as some of the simplest designs can be the most effective. In fact, this enjoyable and fruitful hobby will bring out artistic skills that you never knew you had! It's great to have the satisfaction of making something beautiful and lasting, either for yourself or to give away as a treasured gift.

Begin with a simple project that only requires a steady hand to make lines and dots which, when painted in vivid or subtle colours and repeated in regular shapes, will form surprisingly striking designs for many different pieces of china. As your confidence grows, you will be able to paint or stencil flowers and fruit patterns, and from there you can advance to the flamboyant and colourful designs that people have admired through the ages. Look back to the Victorian era for rich, opulent colours and detailed styles, or try your own versions of the distinctive, colourful designs from the Art Deco period.

My own introduction to painting china came when I was trying out new products in my role as a craft editor for a magazine. I found that I enjoyed it so much that I worked overtime to finish projects as gifts for my family and friends. Car boot sales are now my weekend hunting ground to look for unusual pieces and, if I can't find anything suitable there, I visit my favourite department store for sale bargains. One of my best discoveries was a bargain box of plain white tiles, which I first used to experiment with designs, but later painted as a designer set to revamp a dilapidated bathroom.

The production of new paints, such as the Porcelaine 150 range from Pébéo, means that you can now paint china for everyday use with lasting designs which are safe in contact with food and drink. When dry, ceramic paints, together with the outliners and felt pens in the same series, can be baked onto the china in a domestic oven to make them permanent – even dishwasherproof! The book includes plenty of advice and information on new products so that you can choose the best paints to give your painted china a professional designer look. There are also a number of designs at the back of the book for you to trace and use for the projects in the book.

Step-by-Step Crafts: Painting Ceramics is designed to act as a constant reference source, to give beginners a helping hand to start china painting and to act as an inspiration to all those who have tried this craft before and have enjoyed it. I hope that you will find this an enjoyable pastime and perhaps even the stepping stone to a money-making venture, however small.

Caroline Green

Getting Started

Choosing Ceramics

There are many ways of obtaining ceramics, or chinaware, for painting. One of the best, especially when you are starting out, is to buy cheap items from car boot sales. Slightly imperfect or chipped china is perfect for experimenting with different techniques. Look for an assortment of china, including vases, old plates, dishes and white tiles. Plain white tiles provide an ideal surface for practising. You could test techniques and design ideas on plain tiles and keep a selection of them to use as reference when painting. If some of your ideas are not successful the first time, you can always scrub off the paint with water and try again.

As you become more experienced and your confidence grows, you will want to choose more interesting pieces to paint, such as unusually-shaped tea or coffee pots, small sets of china, or other surprise finds. Hunt out bargains on market stalls, in second-hand shops or charity outlets and ask friends and relatives for odd pieces to revamp. You could also buy inexpensive plates, bowls or jugs and paint them in your favourite designs for everyday use or for special occasions. Try to imagine the potential in any china you see; even a collection of old mugs can be painted with the same design to look like a stylish set.

Items with flat sides are easier to decorate using stamps, traced designs and stencils, as you can lay the pattern directly onto a flat surface. Alternatively, china pieces with curved shapes are ideal for sponged and hand-painted, more intricate, designs. You can choose plain white or cream china, something with a very simple border that you can add to, or plain all-over coloured pieces. White china will show off the paint colours to best effect, but coloured china provides a good base for small decorative borders. If you choose paint colours to complement coloured china you will get some striking results. Black, white and the metallic paint shades will be the most successful as they have excellent covering power.

Make sure the china is clean from grease and dirt before you start painting. All pieces of china, whether old or new, should be cleaned with washing-up liquid, then rinsed off in clear hot water and dried with a clean tea towel.

When you are ready to start painting your designs, always thoroughly degrease the surface of the china using methylated spirits rubbed on with a lint free cloth. This will ensure that the paint adheres to the china properly.

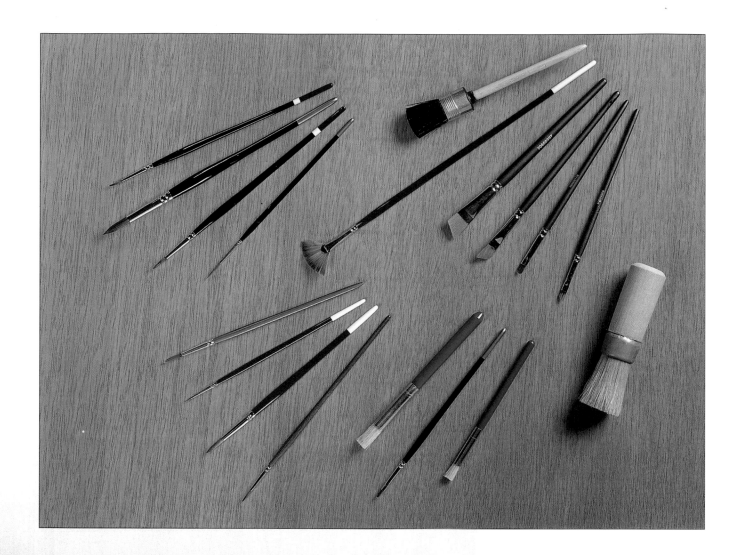

EQUIPMENT

Brushes

With all the different brushes on the market, it can be difficult for the beginner, as well as the experienced hobbyist, to choose the right brush for the job. For the ceramic paints that are used in china painting, watercolour brushes should always be used, except when stencilling (when you should use a stubby bristle brush). Watercolour brushes fall into two types; natural sable or squirrel hair brushes and brushes made of assorted synthetic fibres. Brushes made of natural hair are the best and most expensive, but the synthetic fibre brushes come a very close second and are much cheaper. The water-based paints that are used in this book will wash off very easily from both types of brush. Brushes are available in a range of different shapes and their uses are dealt with in detail on pages 12 and 13.

Chinagraph (coloured wax) pencil

A chinagraph pencil is very useful for marking designs on china as its waxy texture adheres to shiny surfaces. You can buy the pencils in different colours to show up on coloured china. Use them for marking positions for your designs, but always clean off the marks with a cotton bud dipped in methylated spirits prior to painting, or the paint may not adhere properly to the china.

Masking tape

This low-tack tape is very useful for covering areas of china to create bold designs. You can also use it to attach traced patterns or plastic stencils onto china or to provide an accurate measure of the rim of a curved shape as an aid to planning repeat designs. To do this, press a strip of the tape around the rim, cut exactly to size, then remove. You can buy different widths of tape for various uses and also a stretchy

version – useful for creating border designs on bowls and plates – that can be pulled round to mark out curves.

Craft knife

A sharp, pointed craft knife will enable you to cut accurately and cleanly when making your own stencils or cutting masks. It is also ideal for removing areas of dried paint from china before firing.

Sponges

Both natural sea sponges and pieces of synthetic sponge are ideal for applying ceramic paints over a large area, and for creating various mottled textures with paint. Use a natural sponge to produce an open, bold texture and a synthetic sponge for a finer texture.

Cotton buds

Cotton buds are perfect for applying paint in the form of regular dots and for drawing

soft patterns in wet paint. You can also use cotton buds, dipped in a little water, for removing mistakes cleanly, whilst painting.

Cocktail sticks and wooden skewers

Use cocktail sticks and wooden skewers to scratch designs into wet paint. Try using them to make angled and wavy lines or cross-hatched patterns.

Rubber stamps

Detailed designs can be purchased as ready-made rubber stamps. They are ideal for repeated designs giving a pleasing and unique texture where the paint is pressed onto the flat surface of the china.

Neoprene

This is a thin sheet of foam that can be cut into basic shapes with scissors, then glued to card to make your own stamps. Homemade stamps are ideal for reproducing large, repeated patterns.

PAINTS, FELT PENS AND OUTLINERS

There is an ever-increasing choice of ceramic painting products available, ranging from the basic "cold" ceramic colours, which cannot be baked and are purely for decorative projects, to outliners, felt pens and permanent water-based paints that can be baked in a domestic oven. Start by buying a few ceramic paints and outliners and experiment with them to get the feel of china painting.

Water-based ceramic paints

Water-based ceramic paints, such as Porcelaine 150 paints from Pébéo, are primarily for use on china but they also work very well on glassware and terracotta giving a permanent form of decoration when baked in a domestic oven as described below. They are completely safe after baking and so can be used on all kinds of ceramics and chinaware in contact with food and drink. The painted china is also dishwasherproof after baking.

You can apply water-based ceramic paints to china with a brush or sponge to create transparent and semi-opaque designs in a wonderful range of colours. The colours can be mixed together to create new shades and they can also be made paler by diluting with water or filler undercoat. You can vary each colour by adding further coats of paint, to deepen the shade, but make sure you leave each coat to dry for at least ten minutes before re-coating.

You can correct mistakes before firing the design, by wiping off the error with a cotton bud soaked in water, or by scraping it off with a craft knife if the paint has dried hard. Wash out brushes and sponges in clean water immediately after use.

Water-based ceramic paint will dry naturally to a glossy finish, but by adding matt medium to it you can alter this to a matt finish for a different look.

To bake the design on your china, leave the paint to dry for at least 24 hours (it will be touch-dry in about one hour), then place the item in a cold oven and set the temperature to 150°C/300°F/gas mark 2. When the oven reaches this temperature, leave the china to bake for 35 minutes. Switch off the oven and allow the china to cool before removing it from the oven. It is important that the oven temperature is accurate because if the temperature is any lower than specified, the paint will not harden sufficiently to become permanent, and if it is fired at a higher temperature the paint will become permanent but the colour may darken.

Outliners

Outliners, such as those in the Porcelaine 150 range, are water-based paints supplied in a tube with a long thin nozzle. It takes a little practice to become proficient in their use but when you do, they are an invaluable design tool. They produce a slightly raised line with a consistent width, which you can use to make pattern outlines, or they can be used to create dot patterns to enrich painted designs. The outliners come in several colours as well as metallic shades. They can also be baked in the oven so that they become permanent.

Felt pens

New felt pens for ceramics are now available, providing the hobbyist with a wonderful way of drawing fine designs accurately on china. The felt tip transfers the paint to the surface in easy strokes making outlining and even writing really easy. You can also fill in areas quickly and easily leaving few marks to give a smooth, even coating. The paint dries quickly as it is deposited in a fairly thin layer, making multi-coloured designs faster to do.

BASIC
TECHNIQUES

Painting with a round brush

Round watercolour brushes hold the maximum amount of paint and have a pointed end for detailed work. You will find that they are the most useful brushes in your collection with many sizes available in various fibres, both natural and synthetic. Large sizes will produce a beautiful flat wash, while smaller sizes are more suitable for finely detailed work.

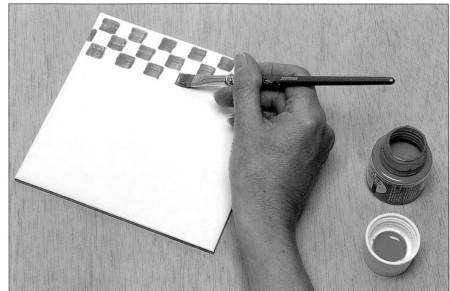

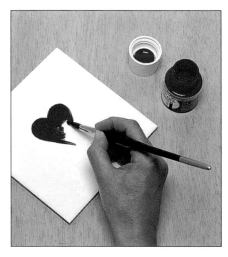

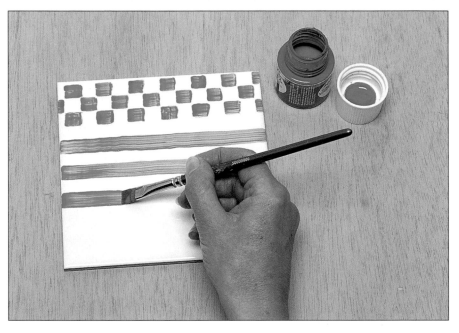

Painting with a flat brush

Flat watercolour brushes are ideal for painting stripes, zigzags and patterns which depend on wide lines of a regular thickness. Choose a width of brush slightly narrower than the line you want and make short strokes to form regular squares for a variety of different patterns (see above right). Use the brush flat to create thick parallel lines and stripes (see centre right). Another variation is to use the brush at an angle, like an italic pen, for thinner lines (see right).

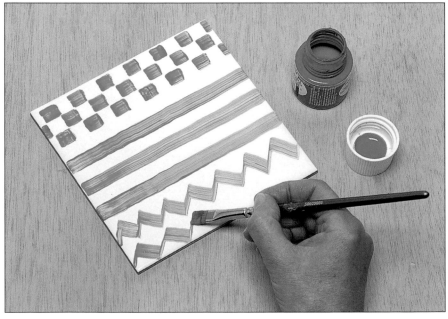

Painting with an angled brush

An angled watercolour brush is similar to a flat brush but the ends of the fibres are cut off at a 45° angle. It is easy to make a flat horizontal wash with regular brush strokes using a large angled brush (see below). Use the end of this brush, dabbed onto a surface in one quick movement, to make daisy-shaped petals (see below centre). You can also form a curved zigzag with this brush for an elegant border or as a foil for simple stripes (see bottom right).

Painting with a long brush

If you need to paint a long thin line, for example when you are painting plant stems, a long-haired round brush is the answer. The fineness of the brush will ensure that the painted line is narrow and the brush will hold a maximum amount of paint so you can paint a long way with one stroke (see above).

Painting with a fan-shaped brush

A fan-shaped brush is one of the more unusual brushes to have in your kit, but it can prove invaluable. Used flat around the edge of an item, it will highlight its outline and emphasize the overall shape (see below). To make a repeated pattern, simply dab the brush onto the surface in rows of semi-circular shapes (see right). The fan-shaped brush stroke can be used to create scales on a fish, clumps of grass or

even an all-over shell pattern. Alternatively, a fan-shaped brush stroke will also create an attractive, soft-edged frame for a stamped, stencilled or painted motif.

Painting with a cotton bud

Decorating with cotton buds is a cross between drawing and painting. The cotton wool tip absorbs just enough paint, making it really easy to control. Start by using this method to make regular round dots and progress to multi-coloured exciting patterns incorporating stripes and squiggles. Replace the cotton bud when the tip gets worn and fluffy.

Sponging

Sponging is a quick way to colour a large area. Depending on the texture of the sponge, you can make a bold pattern, or create a fine speckled effect.

Using a natural sponge

Before using a natural sponge, always wet it and squeeze out all the moisture to make the sponge soft and pliable. Then pour a little paint onto a palette and dip just the tips of the sponge into the paint. Dab off the excess paint on scrap paper, then work on the china with a light dabbing motion (see above). Get rid of excess paint each time you replenish the paint on the sponge to keep the texture even and avoid unsightly blobs. Try a second coat when the first has dried to make a more solid colour or blend two or more colours, by picking up the shades of paints together from the palette. As natural sponges are quite expensive, you should take care of them by rinsing them out in warm water as soon as possible after use.

Using a synthetic sponge

A synthetic sponge will give you an all-over finish with a fine texture, which is ideal for backgrounds and for use as a base for other decorations (see above right). You can also use it for stencilling, masking and shading areas. To imitate the texture of a sea sponge, you can pull out tiny pieces of the synthetic sponge on the flat surface of a cube to change its regular finish. Use cubes of sponge to create a quick and easy check pattern on your china. Simply cut the sponge into small, neat cubes and dip the cubes into the paint for each square of the pattern (see right).

Using outliner

Outliners are water-based and can be made permanent by baking. To start a new tube, unscrew the nozzle and pierce the top of the tube, then quickly replace the nozzle. Squeeze the paint gently down to the tip, then wipe the end of the nozzle on kitchen paper before you begin. It is best to try out this method on a tile or on an old piece of china before working on your finished item, to perfect the technique and to ensure the paint is flowing freely. Touch the paint on to the surface, then lift the nozzle very slightly and squeeze to draw the line of paint along (see below). Let the paint fall on to the surface of the china, forming an even line, rather than dragging the nozzle along, touching the surface,

which will produce an untidy line. The method is similar to icing a cake with a piping nozzle. To make regular tiny dots, simply touch the tip of the nozzle to the china and lift off sharply without squeezing the tube. Keep a tissue handy to wipe the end of the nozzle frequently to keep it clean. When you have finished the design, leave the item to dry for at least 24 hours, then bake in the oven at 150°C/300°F/gas mark 2 for 35 minutes. If you make a mistake, wipe it off immediately with a cotton bud or leave it to dry and scrape it off with the tip of a craft knife before baking.

Stencilling

To stencil a design, first spray the reverse of the stencil or stencil film with stencil mount. Leave this for a few minutes to become tacky, then press the stencil in position on the china. This is particularly useful on curved surfaces to stop the stencil from slipping. For a finely detailed design, use a stencil brush to dab the paint over the stencil, remembering not to use too much paint or it may seep under the edges of the stencil (see below). When you are happy with the paint coverage, lift off

the stencil carefully to reveal the pattern. Continue in this way to complete the design. Leave to dry completely. If there are any stray scraps of paint around the edge, scrape these off with the tip of a craft knife. For a larger design, stencil in the same way but using a synthetic sponge (see bottom of page). This will give you a finer texture and enable you to shade the area with other colours for a three-dimensional look.

Masking designs with paper

Use cut-out paper shapes to mask areas for various patterns. Spray the reverse of the paper shape with spray mount, fix it to the china, then sponge around the edges. Lift the paper to reveal a coloured background with the image in white (see above right).

Masking designs with tape

You can use masking tape to make effective patterns on your china. Regular masking tape can be used in strips, for straight edges, or torn to produce uneven shapes. Stretchy masking tape can be pulled out to make rounded shapes and to follow the edge of plates and dishes for border designs. Simply press the tape in place

where you want the china to remain white (see below). Press the edges down firmly, then sponge lightly around it, in the spaces, aiming for a light, even coverage (see bottom right). Leave until touch-dry, then peel off the tape carefully to reveal the

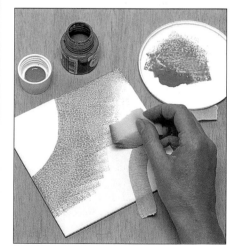

patterns. If some of the paint starts to peel off along with the tape, run the tip of the craft knife along the edge before peeling back the rest of the tape, in order to keep the edge neat. If this happens, it probably means that you have waited too long before trying to remove the tape and the paint has already formed a hard film.

Making designs with masking fluid

To create smaller white patterns use masking fluid to resist the paint. Trace a design, or mark it on the china with a chinagraph pencil. Use a small brush to paint in the shapes with the masking solution. Allow this to dry to a rubbery film, then sponge the background colours all over the surface (see right). Leave this to dry completely, then rub off the dry film of masking fluid with your fingertip to reveal the pattern in white (see far right). You can leave this as it is or paint the shape in a contrasting colour (see Pansy Pasta Bowls on page 68).

Scratching designs into wet colour

To embellish a layer of flat colour, you can add a decorative element by scratching designs through to the surface of the china. Working while the paint is still wet, use the tip of a cotton bud to make wiggles, zigzags and dots (see below). Change the

Stamping

If you have cut your own stamps from neoprene, you can either brush paint onto the surface of the neoprene for a thick layer of paint, or use a sponge roller to apply it thinly. Once you have applied paint to the stamp, press it down onto the china lightly but firmly (see above). Lift the stamp off cleanly to reveal the stamped shape. When using ready-made stamps, apply the paint thinly but evenly with a roller and don't let the stamp slip on the shiny surface of the china as you press it to print. Lift off cleanly as before (see below).

cotton bud as it becomes saturated with paint to keep the pattern well defined. The point of a cocktail stick or wooden skewer will make finer, more detailed patterns (see above) and you can also write in this way. Wipe the wooden tip frequently on clean tissue paper, to remove the excess paint.

Tracing designs

To transfer a traced design, scribble all over the reverse of the tracing with a soft pencil. Turn the tracing back to the other side, tape it to the china and go over the outline with a sharp pointed pencil. Follow the lines of the design carefully to make sure that you don't miss any out. Remove one piece of the tape and lift the tracing off carefully ensuring that you don't smudge the design. Paint the design immediately as the transferred tracing will rub off easily.

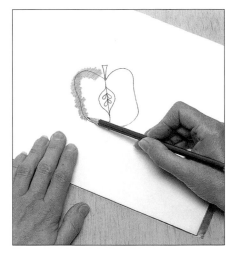

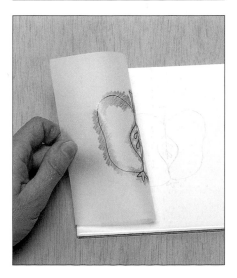

DESIGN INSPIRATION

In addition to using the designs shown in the back of this book, you will find plenty of other sources of inspiration around you. Look at the shape or colour of your china and consider its use, as this may suggest a complementary design and help you to choose a suitable colour or theme. Designs can be adapted to suit your individual china painting style, drawn freehand from embroidery, greetings cards and postcards, giftwrap, wallpaper, fabrics, papier mâché, brochures and magazine features. Start collecting examples of designs that will become the beginnings of your own unique style, but try not to copy slavishly otherwise the designs will not be personal. There are many copyright-free design books that you can use for reference, where you may trace off or photocopy your favourite designs, before trying out different colour schemes. You can enlarge or reduce motifs to fit your china by using a photocopier. This will enable you to design repeat patterns for borders and different sized designs to make a complete set of china. To make your own stencil, copy a simple motif, such as a flower, simplify it and cut out the outline.

1 PROJECT
Red and Yellow Breakfast Set

Choose this quick and easy technique, using simple brush strokes, to start you on the road to more complex china painting. You can paint on either white or plain-coloured china, and experiment with two or more toning colours to create an attractive design. There is no drawing involved as each square of colour is formed with a single brush stroke. Use a large flat brush to paint the squares around the saucer and a medium-sized flat brush for the squares on the cup and on smaller items.

You will need

coral

saffron

A set of breakfast china in a plain colour or white

Methylated spirits

Water-based ceramic paints, such as Porcelaine 150, as shown above

Large flat watercolour brush

Medium-sized flat watercolour brush

1 Wipe all of the breakfast china with methylated spirits to thoroughly degrease the surface ready for painting. Pour some of the coral paint onto a palette and dip the large flat brush into it.

Make regular square brush strokes about 13 mm (½ in) apart around the edge of the saucer. Re-load the brush with paint for each individual square stroke to keep the colour even throughout.

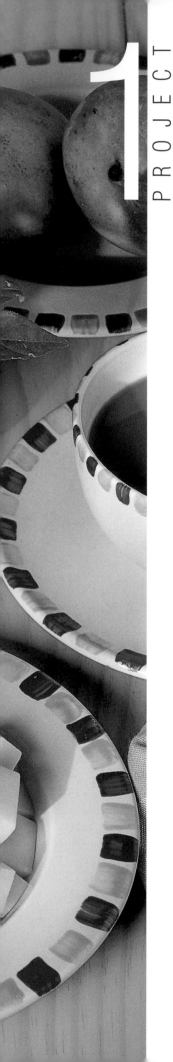

2 Leave the paint until it is touch-dry, then repeat the process using the same size of brush with the saffron paint to form an even row of squares in between the coral ones.

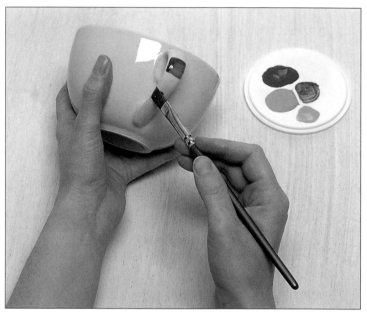

3 When painting the cup, start by painting the handle. Use the same colours and technique, but paint the squares horizontally across the handle. Paint the coral squares first, then fill the spaces in between with the saffron squares. Leave the handle to dry.

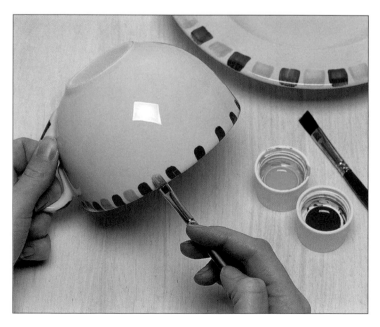

4 For the edge of the cup and other smaller items, scale the pattern down slightly by using a medium-sized brush to create the squares. Holding the cup by its handle, work around the edge of the cup in the same way as you did to paint the plate, using alternate colours spaced evenly.

5 While the paint is still wet, use a piece of dampened kitchen paper, wrapped around your fingertip, to wipe all round the rim of the cup. This will remove any stray scraps of paint that may go over the edge of the cup. Leave all the pieces to dry for 24 hours and bake them following the instructions on page 11.

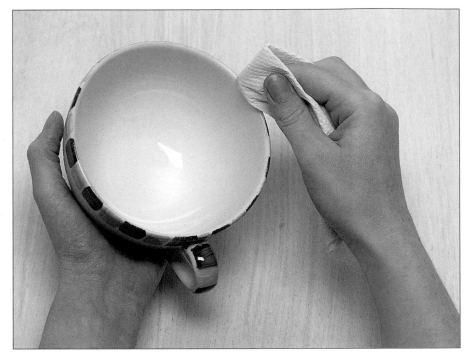

Alternative design:

Vivid blues

Try other colour combinations for this simple but effective design. This version uses vivid turquoise and lapis blue to contrast dramatically with the bright yellow china. Note that as the paints are slightly translucent, the colour of the china will affect the colour of the squares.

2 PROJECT Modern Place Settings

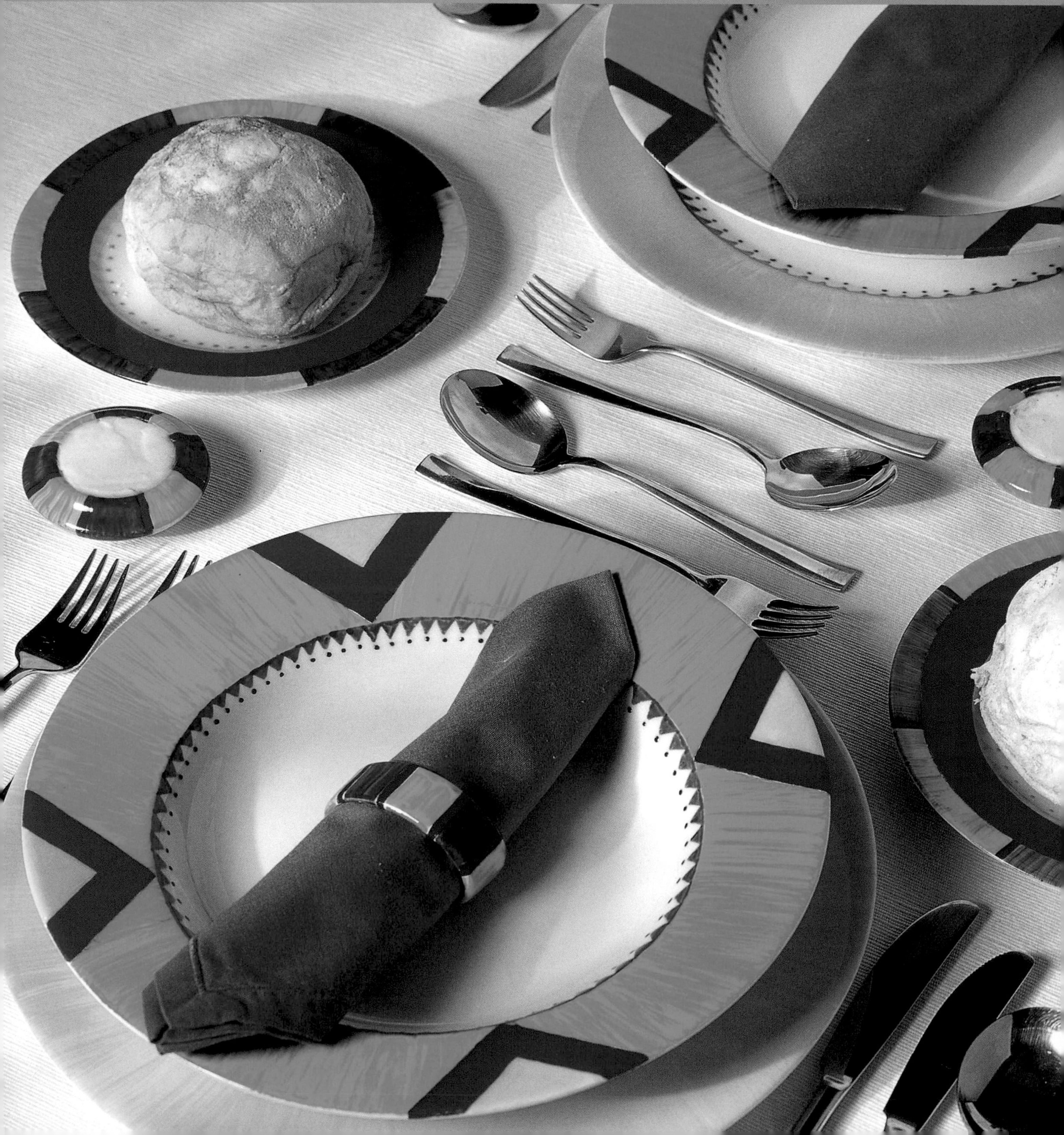

Enliven plain white china place settings by painting them with simple modern designs in vivid colours. Choose plates and bowls with flat rims to enable you to keep the edges of your design professional looking. Complete each setting with a painted butter dish and napkin ring and set your table in different ways to suit the food you have prepared.

1 For the side plates, use a chinagraph pencil and a ruler to make marks around the edge of the plate dividing it into eight equal portions.

You will need

lapis

emerald

coral

citrine yellow

red felt pen

blue felt pen

yellow felt pen

outliner in coral

outliner in Ming blue

outliner in Marseille yellow

A white porcelain side plate, soup bowl, dinner plate, butter dish and napkin ring for each place setting

Chinagraph pencil

Ruler

Stretchy masking tape

Large flat watercolour brush

Water-based ceramic paints, such as Porcelaine 150, as shown above

Felt pens, such as Porcelaine 150, as shown above

Fan-shaped brush

Craft knife

Outliners, such as Porcelaine 150, as shown above

Flat masking tape

Angled flat watercolour brush

2 Use the stretchy masking tape to mask off the inner edge of the rim of the plate. To make the tape curve round to follow the shape of the plate, stretch the top edge of the tape to flatten out the ribbing and line up the bottom of the tape along the inner rim of the plate. Press the tape in place all round, smoothing the tape in position as you go. Make sure the two ends of tape line up where they meet.

3 Using the large flat brush and the lapis blue, paint the outer edge in alternate sections around the edge of the plate. Place the tip of the brush over the edge of the tape and brush out towards the edge of the plate to create even, radiating brush strokes. Paint all the blue sections, then paint the alternate ones in the same way, using the emerald paint and avoiding the chinagraph lines. Leave to dry, then wipe off the chinagraph pencil.

4 Use the red felt pen to draw lines to replace the chinagraph pencil lines between the blocks of lapis and emerald paint. Carefully peel off the masking tape, then paint the inner edge of the rim, using the coral paint. Place the tip of the brush at the edge of the painted area and make a stroke towards the centre of the plate. You can let the paint go over the inner edge of the rim, then scrape it off later, when the paint is dry or, if you prefer, mask the inner edge with tape as before. Paint the napkin rings and butter dishes to go with the side plates.

5 For the dinner plate, use the fan-shaped brush to paint the rim with the citrine yellow, aiming for even, radiating brush strokes as before. Leave the paint to dry, then use a craft knife to scrape off the uneven inner edge around the rim of the plate (as shown in detail above). Hold the blade of the craft knife at the same angle as you go round the plate to make a smooth, even edge.

6 Mark a border of small triangles all round the inner edge of the rim using the red felt pen. Draw the outline first then fill in the centre of each. Leave these to dry, then use the red outliner to make a tiny dot at the apex of each triangle. Use this method to decorate the inner edge of the side plate in yellow.

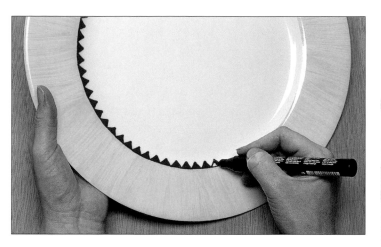

artist's tip

If your first coat of paint looks very thin, use a hairdryer to speed up the drying process so that you can apply a second coat of paint in the same way for a deeper shade.

7 For the soup plate, divide the rim into four using the chinagraph pencil and a ruler as for the side plates. Use short strips of flat masking tape to mask large triangles at these four points. Using the fan-shaped brush, paint the rim of the plate in emerald, as before, painting outwards across the rim. Leave the rim to dry, then remove the tape and scrape off any excess paint from the inner edge of the plate.

8 Paint the two outer edges of the triangles in red using the angled flat brush to get into the corners neatly. You may need two coats of paint to achieve the depth of colour you require. Leave this to dry, then paint the remaining space in between (the inner triangle) in yellow. Leave the inner triangle to dry, then paint a triangle and dot border in blue using the felt pen and outliner. Leave all the pieces to dry for 24 hours, then fire in the oven following the manufacturer's instructions.

3 PROJECT Sponged Cups and Saucers

E legant white porcelain cups and saucers can be given an ornate, antique appearance using sponged mixed colours and gold decoration. The varied all-over shade is created with two-colour sponging while the outer edges are decorated with two shades of gold in a striking dot pattern using outliners. You could decorate a porcelain teapot or coffeepot and a milk jug in the same way to match.

You will need

lapis

ruby

outliner in vermeil

outliner in pale gold

White porcelain cups and saucers

Water-based ceramic paints, such as Porcelaine 150, as shown above

Palette

Small natural sponge

Kitchen towel

Outliners, such Porcelaine 150 outliners, as shown above

1 Clean the porcelain cups and saucers thoroughly. Pour a small amount of ruby and lapis paint onto your palette. Wet the sponge to soften it and squeeze out all the water. Dip one side of the sponge into both colours at once and dab it on the palette to mix them slightly.

2 Holding the cup by the top and bottom edges, sponge the paints over the surface. Leave the handle free of paint and replenish the sponge as necessary. Try to cover the surface without mixing the two colours into one flat shade.

3 Moisten a piece of kitchen paper and wrap it around your fingertip. Use this to wipe the top rim of the cup leaving it free of paint. Leave the paint until it is touch-dry.

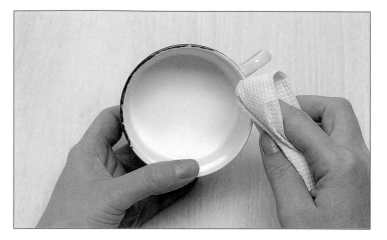

4 Tear off a small piece of the sponge and use this to colour the handle in the same way, reaching into the corners and under the handle with the tip of the sponge. Sponge all over the saucers with the whole sponge in the same way and leave the paint to dry until it is hard.

5 Using the vermeil outliner, make a row of tiny dots around the edge of the saucer. Draw three dots vertically below each pair of dots and join two of these into a loop with two more dots (see the detail on the next page). Continue in this way around the saucer to form a regular pattern.

6 Using the same outliner, draw a large dot between each loop of tiny dots, then draw an outline diamond shape below each large dot. Leave until the outliner is dry.

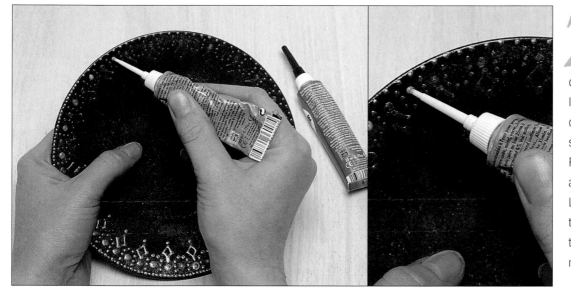

7 Using the pale gold outliner, draw tiny dots between the darker gold dots. Leave to dry, then draw a large dot inside each loop and a tiny dot at the point of each diamond shape to complete the pattern. Repeat this design around the cups, a little way down from the top edge. Leave all the china to dry for two or three days as the outliner is quite thick. Bake in the oven following the manufacturer's instructions.

Notice the subtle difference between the pale and the dark gold outliner paint that forms the delicate pattern of diamonds and dots in this unusual, ornate design.

painting ceramics/project 3

Sponged China
Gallery

Top shelf, left to right:

Two-tone bowl
This ridged bowl lends itself to easy two-tone sponging. Use a fine-textured synthetic sponge to apply lilac paint all over and leave to dry. Then lightly sponge the rim and the ridges with blue.

Golden shell dish
This attractive shell-shaped soap dish was made using the same technique as above, but with two different shades of gold to give a rich metallic sheen.

Oriental urn
The urn is sponged all over with a very fine synthetic sponge in pink water-based paint and left to dry. Use a very open-textured natural sponge to apply a haze of gold over the top.

Middle shelf, left to right:

Brilliant pink plant pot
Sponge pink paint all over the outside of the pot as for the urn. Leave to dry and sponge the inside in gold as a contrast.

Blue and green bowl
Use a natural sponge to cover the outside and inside rim of the bowl with an open-textured coating of blue water-based paint. Leave to dry, then use a synthetic sponge to apply a fine coating of green paint over the inner rim and lower half of the bowl, leaving the central area clear as a contrast.

Lower shelf, left to right:

Watercolour cup and saucer
For a light, delicate look use a synthetic sponge to apply diluted blue and green water-based paint all over the cup and saucer. This also makes a perfect base for further painted decorations.

Blue and white jug and hearts bowl
Cover the top and lower rims of the jug with flexible masking tape and sponge blue water-based paint all over it, using an open-textured natural sponge. For the hearts bowl, cut out four heart shapes from wide masking tape and stick them on the bowl at equal distances. Mask the top edge and sponge the bowl as for the blue and white jug. Peel off the tape when the paint is dry and sponge the hearts and the top edge with yellow paint using a fine synthetic sponge.

Moulded China
Gallery

All-over pattern jug
Try this speedy technique for an all-over colour effect that highlights the jug's fruity pattern. Using a large brush, apply blue paint all over the jug, except the handle. While the paint is still wet, wipe over the surface with a pad of slightly moist kitchen paper to remove some of the paint on the top surface of the china, leaving colour in the recesses. Wipe the edges of the jug clean and leave to dry. Sponge the handle to match.

Tiny flower basket
Bring out the pretty pattern on this miniature china basket by highlighting areas of the design in leaf green, using a small round brush. Carefully follow the shapes moulded on to the surface of the basket, wiping off any mistakes with the tip of a cotton bud.

Middle shelf, left to right:

Daisy planter
Using a small piece of synthetic sponge, colour the background of this pot in bright yellow, avoiding the raised daisies. Leave to dry, then paint the edges of each petal in pink and the flower centres in yellow, using a fine round brush.

Classic planter
Paint the acanthus leaf shapes in deep aquamarine water-based ceramic paint using a round brush, with the brush strokes fanning out from the centre of the leaf. Leave to dry. Paint the trellis background in a paler colour. Finally sponge the top and bottom edges in the same shade to complete the design.

Lower shelf, left to right:

Celery pot
Use a quick, freehand blend of different greens, colouring this celery pot to look like the real thing. Work with long sweeping strokes to shade the moulding naturally and paint the roots at the base with tiny, thin strokes using a small brush.

Rose bowl
Sponge all over the outside of the bowl with pale leaf green water-based ceramic paint. While the paint is still wet, wipe off the surface of each raised flower. Leave to dry and then paint each flower with a random swirl of red and orange paint.

Topiary Tree Plant Pots

eat topiary trees make a smart design that will unite a random collection of white china plant pots. Stencilling is the easiest method of reproducing these detailed designs and the use of different sizes and styles of tree will enable you to fit almost any shape of pot.

You will need

malachite
emerald
amber
topaz

White china plant pots
Mylar stencil film
Fine, black, waterproof felt tip pen
Craft knife
Cutting mat or thick card
Scissors
Cardboard box (for spraying)
Stencil mount spray glue
Water-based ceramic paints,
such as Porcelaine 150, as
shown above
Palette
Cotton buds
Small pieces of synthetic sponge
Small round watercolour brush

1 Clean the china plant pots thoroughly. Trace off the topiary designs from page 93 onto pieces of the Mylar stencil film, using the black felt tip pen. Cut out the stencils with a craft knife, working on a cutting mat or card. Trim the edge of the film with scissors so that it fits your pot.

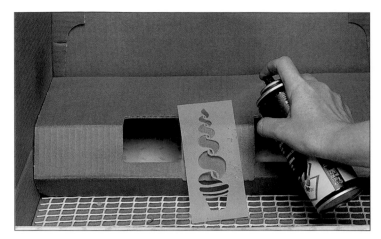

2 Using a cardboard box as a protective spraying booth, spray the reverse of the stencils with a fine coating of stencil mount glue. Leave this to go tacky before using the stencil. This will help the stencil to stay in position on the china, even on a shiny, curved surface.

3 Place one stencil centrally on one side of a plant pot. Pour a little of the two green paints onto the palette and mix the malachite and emerald together with the tip of a cotton bud. Dab the paint over the upper tree part of the stencil onto the pot. This will give a textured finish to your design. You could also use a piece of sponge to stencil the colours for a smoother, shaded finish.

4 Mix some of the amber and topaz paint to create a mixed terracotta shade, then using a clean cotton bud apply this colour to the pot and trunk part of the stencil design. Leave for a few moments for the paint to become slightly tacky.

5 Lift off the stencil film carefully to reveal the tree design beneath. Continue stencilling designs on the flat surfaces around the pot in the same way. Use any combination of the tree designs to suit the different shaped pots. You can enlarge and reduce these designs with a photocopier and cut out the stencils as needed.

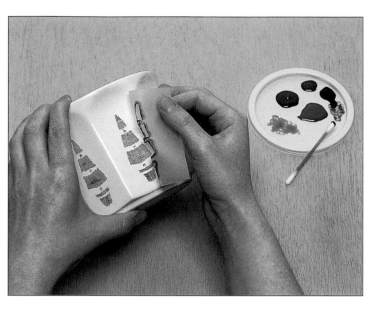

6 To complete the design, paint a trio of small hand-painted leaves in the triangular spaces around the top edge of the pot using a small watercolour brush. Use the same green shades to tone in with the main stencilled designs. Leave to dry for at least 24 hours, then fire the pot in the oven following the manufacturer's instructions.

artist's tip

You may find that if you use too much paint on the stencil, some may seep under the stencil and spoil the outline of your design. If this happens, leave the paint to dry for a few hours and then scrape away the excess around the edges using the tip of a craft knife.

Safari Teapot and Mugs

I f you love the bold fashion statement of animal prints, why not create a set of mugs and matching teapot in the exciting shades and patterns of the jungle. The leopard print design is first sponged, then stencilled with an all-over pattern and the tiger and zebra designs are hand-painted with a watercolour brush following traced designs.

1 Clean the china mugs and the teapot thoroughly. Pour the saffron and calcite paints onto a palette and dip in a piece of synthetic sponge. Dab the sponge on the palette to mix the colours slightly.

2 Sponge the two paints over the surface of the china, leaving the handle free of paint so that you can still hold it. Cover the surface completely keeping a mottled mix of the two colours.

You will need

saffron

calcite

black

White china mugs and teapot

Water-based ceramic paints, such as Porcelaine 150, as shown above

Palette

Synthetic sponge

Kitchen towel

Fine, waterproof felt tip pen

Mylar stencil film

Hot stencil cutter

A tile or melamine board to cut stencil

Scissors

Stencil mount spray glue

Small stencil brush

Medium-sized watercolour brush

3 Using a moistened piece of kitchen towel wrapped around your fingertip, wipe the rim of the mug to clean off any excess paint. Leave the paint until touch-dry, then using a small piece of sponge, colour the handle in the same way, reaching under the handle with the tip of the sponge. Sponge all over the teapot and lid in the same way and leave the paint to dry hard.

4 For the leopard skin design, use the felt tip pen to trace off the design on page 92 onto a piece of Mylar stencil film slightly larger than the depth of the mug. Using a hot cutter and following the manufacturer's instructions, cut out the shapes on a tile or piece of melamine board. Trim the edge of the stencil film with scissors so that it will fit your mug, then spray the reverse with stencil mount and leave to go tacky.

5 Position your stencil on the mug to line up with the lower edge. Pour a little black paint into a palette, then dip the tips of the stencil brush into the paint and dab off the excess on a piece of scrap paper. Dab the paint through the holes in the stencil to create the design. Use the paint sparingly to retain the texture of the brush for a furry effect.

6 Leave the paint to dry for a few moments, then lift off the stencil film carefully to reveal the design beneath. Reposition the stencil and continue in this way to cover the whole mug. Take care not to smudge the paint as you work.

Tiger stripes on the teapot. Paint the characteristic wavy lines in varying widths on a sponged golden brown background for a realistic furry finish.

7 For the tiger skin pattern, follow the design on page 92. You can paint the design freehand using the pattern as a reference or, alternatively, trace off the shapes and transfer them to the painted surface. Use black paint with the medium-size watercolour brush.

artist's tip
When working on areas that are awkward to stencil, such as around the handle and on the curved rim, where the stencil film will not bend or fit, use the tip of a cotton bud dipped in the paint to imitate the leopard skin pattern.

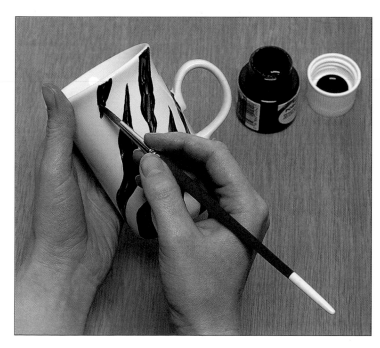

8 For the zebra pattern, paint the wide lines following the designs on page 92 in black on a plain white mug. The zebra stripes are best painted at an angle to follow around the shape of the mug for a natural look. You may need two coats to make a really dense black, so let the first coat dry before adding more paint. Leave the paint to dry for at least 24 hours, then bake the china following the manufacturer's instructions.

Mugs
Gallery

Top shelf, left to right:

Two-tone heart mug
Sponge blue paint around a heart-shaped paper mask. Leave the paint to dry, then sponge the heart in a contrasting colour.

Torn stripes mug
Tear strips of wide masking tape and press them randomly onto the mug. Sponge around the stripes and peel off the tape when the paint is touch-dry.

Circle-sponged mug
Stick file hole reinforcements around your mug, sponge it in pale green and colour in the centres of each circle.

Art Deco scene mug
(Artist: Judy Balchin)
For this Clarice Cliff-style mug, trace the design, then paint on two or three coats of each colour. Leave to dry, then use black outliner to define the shapes. Finally, sponge the top and bottom edges.

Spots and stripes mug
(Artist: Judy Balchin)
For a freehand design of spots, checks and stripes, paint the main areas in your favourite shades, leave to dry and add the details with felt pens.

Middle shelf, left to right:

Modern art mug
Paint a small yellow diamond shape on the side of the mug. Working outwards, paint diamond outlines of varying thickness in blue, red and green. Leave to dry, then outline the shapes with black outliner.

Watercolour mug
Pour some blue and green paint onto a palette, add a little water and sponge this over the mug to achieve a watery texture.

Brush work mug
Create this textured surface by roughly painting a single colour using a large brush. This effect looks attractive on its own or could be used as a background for further painting.

1950s style mug (Artist: Judy Balchin)
Use paper shapes to mask out random circles and triangles. Sponge yellow paint all over the mug and use orange at the top edge. Leave to dry, then peel off the masks and paint the centres of the circles. Paint the triangles in green, with three brush strokes. Paint on the red squiggles and sponge the handle in blue.

Patchwork mug (Artist: Judy Balchin)
Divide the mug into three rows of squares and paint each square to look like a piece of blue patterned fabric. Leave to dry, then carefully sponge the top and lower edges and the handle in yellow. When the paint is completely dry, draw the dividing lines and tiny stitches with black outliner to look like hand-stitched patchwork.

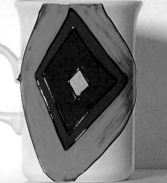

Lower shelf, left to right:

Dotty mug
To achieve this quick and easy pattern, dip the end of a wine bottle cork into blue paint and use it to stamp large spots all over the mug.

Lemon mug
Brush paint a large lemon on to the side of the mug in yellow and add leaves in pale green. Use the same green on a medium-sized round brush to create the border pattern of single flat strokes of the brush.

Purple and gold mug
This rich purple colour is made by sponging red and blue paint together all over the mug. Leave to dry, then use gold outliner to make intricate dotted patterns around the top.

Pink heart mug (Artist: Judy Balchin)
Try this pretty, modern design using felt pens for china in pink and black. Add random areas of gold paint to the background, using a flat brush to make perfect squares.

Cherry ripe mug
This easy design can be painted freehand in water-based paints. Paint the cherry pairs first, then add the stalks and leaves to complete the design.

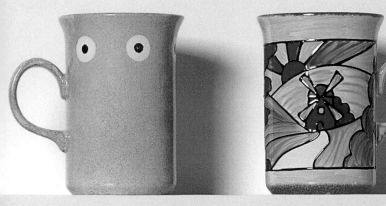

6 PROJECT
Mexican Wave Tiles

Paint a set of tiles in vivid blue and turquoise to brighten up your bathroom. The basic wave design is sponged and then combed in wavy lines. These tiles are arranged with a row of striking star tiles with wavy side panels. Additional tiles featuring stencilled and masked designs are interspersed with the wave tiles to add extra interest over the whole wall.

You will need

lapis blue

turquoise

Plain white tiles

Methylated spirits

Stiff card

Craft knife and cutting mat

Water-based ceramic paints, such as Porcelaine 150, as shown above

Palette

Small pieces of synthetic sponge

Tracing paper

Pencil

Piece of neoprene, about 9 cm (3½ in) square

Scissors

All-purpose glue

Cotton buds

Mylar stencil film

Black felt tip pen

Spray mount

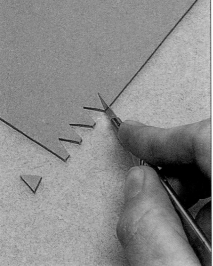

1 Clean all the tiles thoroughly by wiping them with methylated spirits. For the basic wave design, cut a piece of stiff card about 9 x 13 cm (3½ x 5 in). Using a craft knife, cut small V-shaped notches along one short edge of the card to make a comb.

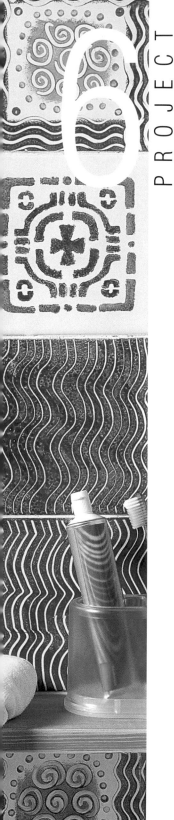
2 Pour some of the lapis blue paint onto a clean palette. Dip a piece of synthetic sponge into the paint and dab this all over one of the tiles. Try to make an even coating that completely covers the white tile.

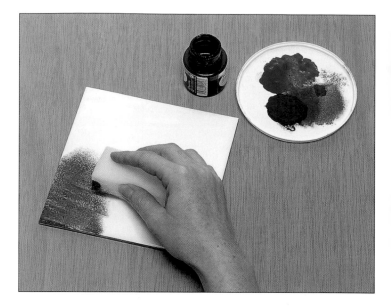

3 Whilst the paint is still wet, use the comb to make a wavy panel across the top half of the tile. Work in one smooth wavy movement to avoid smudges, and ensure that the pattern goes right over the sides of the tile.

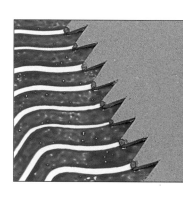

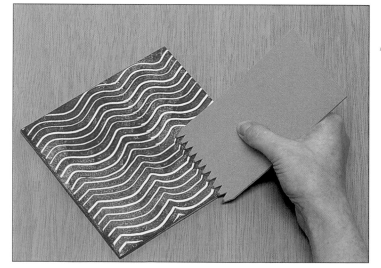

4 Wipe the edge of the comb to remove any excess paint and make a second wavy panel to follow the shape of the first, covering the remainder of the tile. This completes your basic wave design. Set each tile aside to dry for 24 hours before firing.

5 To create the star tile design, first trace off the star shape on page 93 and transfer it to a piece of neoprene. Cut out the star shape with scissors and glue it centrally onto a 10 cm (4 in) square of card.

6 Using the synthetic sponge, apply a layer of lapis blue paint to the surface of the stamp, then press the stamp centrally onto a tile. Lift off carefully and set the tile aside to dry. To make the wavy border, follow the instructions in step 7.

Mexican wave pattern on the tile. If you use the comb carefully, continuing the lines neatly across the tile, the resulting wave pattern will have a mesmerizing effect on the eye.

7 To make a wavy border on a tile, first cut a smaller card comb about 4 cm (1½ in) wide, as before, then sponge on a band of lapis blue paint along the top and lower edges of the tile. Use the small card comb to make wavy borders as before. Repeat this step to complete the side borders of the tile and leave the tile until it is touch-dry.

8 When the borders are dry, sponge the central area of the tile in turquoise. While the sponged paint is still wet, use a dry cotton bud to draw several spirals in the centre of the tile.

9 To complete this design, dip a clean cotton bud into the turquoise paint and make dots around the central motif and one in each corner.

10 With a black felt tip pen, trace the two designs on page 93 through the Mylar stencil film, then cut them out using a craft knife. Spray the reverse side of the stencils with stencil mount and place each stencil centrally on a tile. Dip the sponge in a mix of blue and turquoise paint and stencil the patterns onto the tiles.

artist's tip
If you smudge any paint while decorating your tiles, dip a new cotton bud in water and use it to clean up around the edges of your designs before firing.

11 Lift off the stencil carefully to reveal the pattern beneath. Leave the tiles to dry for at least 24 hours, then bake according to the instructions on page 11 and leave to cool in the oven. When the tiles are cold, attach them to the bathroom walls using a mixture of tile cement and grout.

7 PROJECT Serving Dish and Spoon

deal as a salad or fruit bowl, this dish with matching
serving spoon is hand-painted freely without using a
pattern. The swirling organic design is applied with sweeping
brush strokes in bright, vivid colours for a fresh summery
look. In contrast to the smooth pattern on the inside of the
dish, the base of the bowl is decorated with a two colour
texture applied with a scrunched-up rag.

You will need

pale green

yellow

dark green

White china dish and spoon

Water-based ceramic paints, such
as Ceramica, as shown above

Large round watercolour brush

Medium-sized round watercolour
brush

Tin for supporting the dish

Soft cloth

Small piece of clean cotton cloth

Palette

Kitchen paper

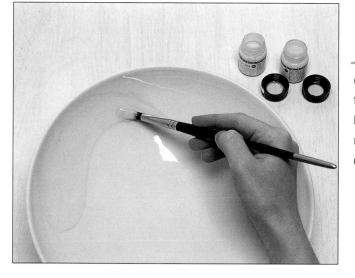

1 Clean the china thoroughly. Start by painting three large paisley or teardrop shapes around the inner rim of the dish using the pale green paint. Use the large brush and make smooth sweeping brush strokes. These three shapes should be roughly the same size, leaving an open circular space in the centre of the bowl.

2 Leave the pale green paint until it is touch-dry, then paint the background and the rim in yellow with the large round brush. Paint quickly and make the brush strokes follow the edges of the curved shapes made by the pale green paint. Leave the bowl overnight until it is dry. You could speed up the drying process by using a hairdryer on a warm setting.

3 Using the darker green and the medium-sized brush, paint a spiral line in the centre of each paisley shape. Decorate each spiral with two or three dots in the same colour. Finally paint a large spiral in the centre of the dish in the same colour. Leave the bowl overnight to dry as before.

4 Turn the dish over and balance it on a tin covered with a soft cloth so that the dish is not touching the work surface. Pour out a little yellow paint onto a palette, scrunch up the small piece of cloth and dip it into the yellow paint. Dab this randomly over the outside of the dish and leave until the paint is touch-dry. Then repeat the process with the darker green paint to create a two-tone textured finish.

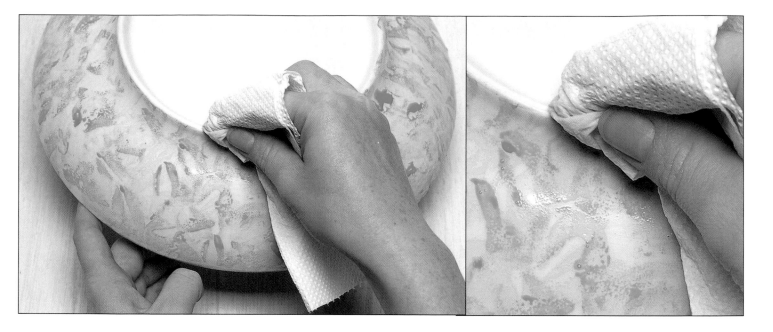

5 While the darker green paint is still wet, use a piece of moistened kitchen paper to wipe around the lower rim of the bowl to clean off any excess paint.

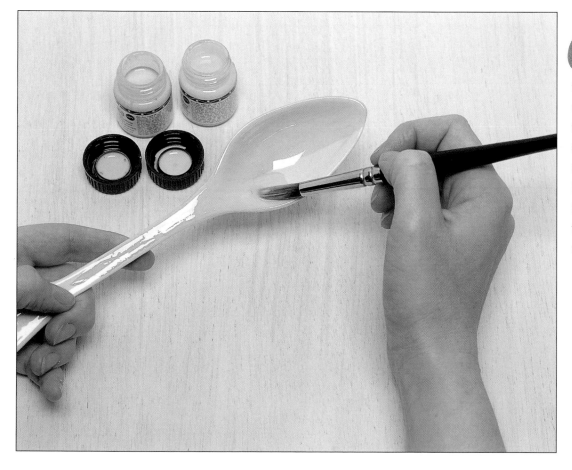

6 Paint the spoon to go with the dish, following similar curved shapes and spirals to those painted on the bowl. Start with one end of the spoon, leave this to dry, then paint the other end, so that you always have a dry part of the spoon to hold whilst painting. Leave the paint to dry for at least 24 hours, then bake the dish and the spoon in the oven following the manufacturer's instructions.

Shell Design Bathroom Set

A simple shell design, chosen to evoke the seaside, is ideal for decorating bathroom accessories. Vivid turquoise will go with most bathroom schemes and the stencil technique is quick and easy to perfect. Try out the design in a range of colours, or use another motif for a different setting. The shell design is also ideal for bathroom tiles.

You will need

turquoise

ivory white

White china toothmug, toothbrush holder, basket, soap dish and liquid soap dispenser

Mylar stencil film

Pencil or fine waterproof felt tip pen

Craft knife

Cutting mat or thick card

Scissors

Stencil mount spray glue

Water-based ceramic paints, such as Porcelaine 150, as shown above

Palette

Synthetic sponge

Small stencil brush

1 Clean the china thoroughly. Trace off the shell and border designs from page 94 onto separate pieces of the stencil film, using the pencil or felt tip pen.

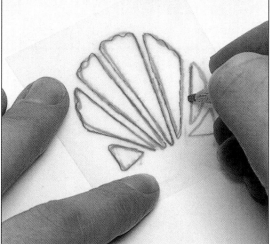

2 Carefully cut out the stencil using the craft knife and cutting mat or card. Trim around the edges of the film with scissors so that they will fit the china and spray the reverse of the stencil with a fine coating of stencil mount glue. Leave this to go tacky before applying the stencil to the china. This will help the stencil to stay in position, even on a shiny, curved surface.

3 Position the shell stencil onto a flat side of one of the china accessories. Pour a little of each colour onto the palette, then dip a small piece of the sponge into the paint. Mix the paint colours together to make a pale turquoise, then dab the paint through the stencil onto the china. Stencil all over the shell shape and leave for a few moments until the paint is touch-dry.

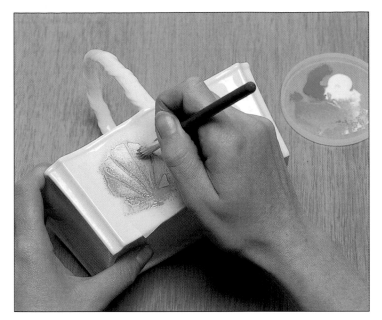

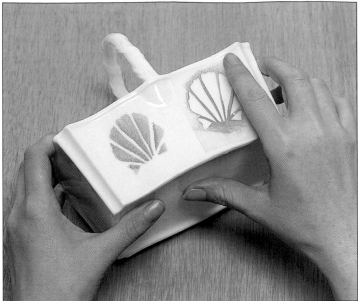

4 Dip the tips of a clean, dry stencil brush into the turquoise paint, not mixed with any white paint, and apply this darker colour sparingly over the stencil to add shading to the overall design.

5 Lift off the stencil film carefully to reveal the design and re-position it ready for the next part of the design. Continue stencilling the shell design around the flat sides of the pot in the same way.

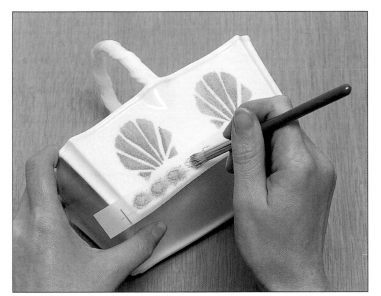

6 Stencil the tiny shell border in the same way but using the brush to push the paint through the smaller design. Decorate the other items, leave all pieces to dry for 24 hours and bake them in the oven following the manufacturer's instructions.

Alternative design:

Abstract pattern

This elegant china pot, suitable as a container for cotton wool or cotton buds, has been painted with an abstract stencilled pattern. The lid and base of the pot have a dotted border, created using a cocktail stick dipped in paint. You can draw your own abstract designs, cut them from stencil film, then transfer them to any container of your choice, in any colour you wish.

Plates and Bowls
Gallery

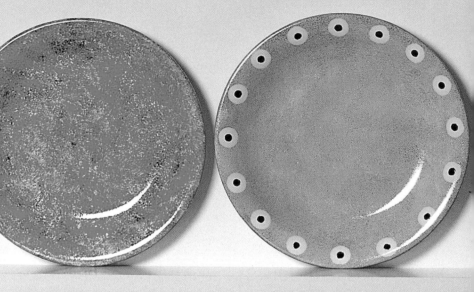

Top shelf, left to right:

Sea blue
All-over sponging in two shades – blue and emerald green – gives this vibrant colour a fine-textured finish.

Circle border
Use file hole reinforcements for this sponged plate. The centres of the circles were painted later.

Linear look
Alternate double stripes in turquoise and lime green felt pen are drawn all round the well-defined rim of this plate. Wiggly pen lines and dots are drawn in alternate spaces.

Star-struck
Stencil the central star, then paint tiny stars around the edge of the plate with a small brush. Decorate with gold outliner.

Jester
Evenly spaced diamonds and spots in black outliner decorate the edge of this dish. Fill the dried outlines with bold colours.

Middle shelf, left to right:

On the spot
A cork, dipped into mixed blue and green water-based paint, is ideal for the quick and simple spots on this plate.

Blue swirl
Paint the whole plate using slightly diluted turquoise water-based paint and a large flat brush. Leave to dry, then draw small spirals onto the plate with blue felt pen.

Brush stroke bowls
Use a flat brush to paint the indentations on these bowls. The contrasting squares around the rim are made with single strokes of the same brush. Finally, sponge the lower edge.

Torn stripes
Mask a plate with torn strips of masking tape and sponge it with blue paint. Leave until touch-dry and gently pull off the tape.

Brushed stripes
(Artist: Judy Balchin)
Paint wide, even stripes in red, yellow, green and orange across the plate, using a wide flat brush. Leave to dry. Paint wiggly lines and dots over the top of some stripes.

Lower shelf, left to right:

Cherry ripe border
Use a small round brush to paint pairs of cherries. Paint the stalks and leaves for each pair with a very fine brush.

Lemon zest
The pair of lemons are painted in pale yellow water-based paint and left to dry. Dabs of darker yellow add texture. Paint the leaves and stem before adding the border.

Rose tea plate
This old-fashioned tea plate is embellished with a large rose painted in quick strokes with a round brush. The petals and leaves were defined later with red and green felt pens for using on china.

Roses all the way
(Artist: Judy Balchin)
Painted in a similar way to the tea plate, these smaller roses and the leaves outlined in black have a bolder, more 1930s look. The edge of the plate is sponged pink.

Spinning soup plates
These soup plates were centred on a cake icing turntable, then lines of diluted water-based paint were applied to the spinning plate. Leave to dry and apply a second colour.

Vibrant lilies (Artist: Judy Balchin)
Trace your design onto the plate, follow the lines with a black outliner and leave to dry. Paint in the flowers, leaves and background with water-based paints using a round brush.

Plain white plates take on a new look when they are decorated with stencilled fruit designs. Create a varied orchard fruit set with apples and pears in subtle greens, yellows and pinks, or design your own tropical fruit stencils for a more exotic theme. Using special felt pens, you can draw in details such as pips and leaf veins to add extra interest to the main designs.

You will need

olivine

malachite

citrine

ivory white

fuchsia

saffron

pale green felt pen

dark green felt pen

White china plates

Mylar stencil film

Fine, black waterproof felt tip pen

Craft knife

Cutting mat or thick card

Stencil mount spray glue

Water-based ceramic paints, such as Porcelaine 150, as shown above

Palette

Small pieces of synthetic sponge

Felt pens for china as shown above

Scissors

1 Clean the china plates thoroughly. Trace off the apple and pear outlines from page 94 onto separate pieces of stencil film, using the felt tip pen.

2 Cut out the stencil shapes with the craft knife, working on a cutting mat or piece of thick card. Spray the reverse of the stencils with a fine coating of the stencil mount glue and leave this to go tacky before using the stencil.

3 Place the stencil centrally onto a plate. Pour a little of the yellow and green paints onto the palette, then dip the edge of a piece of the sponge into the paints, mixing the colours a little. Dab the paint through the leaf part of the stencil.

4 Mix some white and yellow paint together on a palette, then use a clean piece of sponge to stencil all over the apple. Lift off the stencil film carefully and leave the paint to dry thoroughly for several hours.

5 Following the design on page 94, draw the outline and core with pips on the apple design using the pale green felt pen. Leave to dry, then draw the leaf veins and fill in the centre of the pips with the dark green pen. When you have sponged the pear design on a separate plate, you can finish this off with similar details.

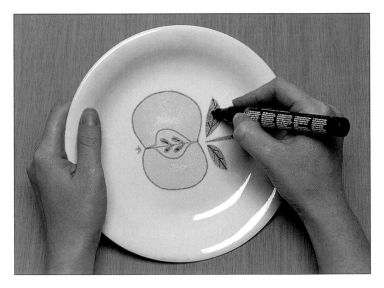

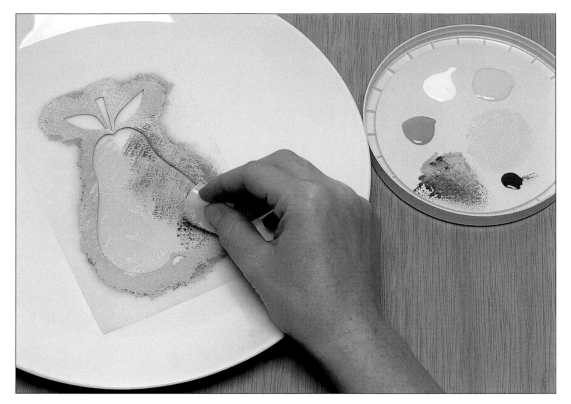

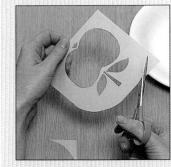

6 If you want to show just the outside of the fruit, stencil in the same way but add more colours to resemble a ripe fruit. The red and orange should be sponged on lightly after the pale yellow is touch-dry. Leave all the paint to dry for at least 24 hours, then fire in the oven following the manufacturer's instructions.

artist's tip

Using scissors, trim the corners of the stencil film so that the film will fit into the centre of your plates. This will enable the stencil to lie flat on the china and make the stencilling easier.

variation

To add a coloured edge to your plates, dip the tips of a fan brush into a mixture of the same paints you have used for the stencilling, then apply the paint sparingly to the edge of the plate to make a soft feathery texture all the way around the rim.

Jugs and Vases
Gallery

Top shelf, left to right:

Tiny tulips jug
Give a plain white jug a charming floral style with tiny brush painted tulips in many different colours.

Doodle design jug
Use a black felt pen for china to doodle a bold design all over a plain jug, letting the lines form islands. When the lines are dry, fill some areas with a bold colour.

Jester jug
Use the facets on this jug to help you paint a bold design. The lower area is sponged to give an even colour, and the triangles are painted with dots of a contrasting colour, applied with a cotton bud.

Spiral design flower holder
This unusual flower holder has been decorated with diluted paint while being rotated on a cake icing turntable. Centre the item and fix it with kneadable adhesive. It takes only moments to apply the paint with a large round brush.

Middle shelf, left to right:

Striped jug
A tiny square jug, probably left over from an old tea set, can be turned into a little flower jug ideal for displaying bright garden flowers.

Aqua triangle jug
Another little jug takes on a different look with a modern triangle design quickly drawn on with felt pens for china in shades of blue and green.

Mosaic vase
Dip a small flat brush into blue paint and paint short square strokes in a circular fashion to achieve a mosaic effect.

Bud vase trio
Three bud vases sponged in brilliant mauve and yellow look good displayed together with a single bloom in each.

Cubist guitar jug
Draw a bold design of abstract guitars in black felt pen for china. When dry, paint the design with red and yellow in flat areas and add stripes and spots.

Lower shelf, left to right:

Floral cameo vase
Cut out an oval paper mask, spray with adhesive and attach it centrally to the front of the vase. Sponge the vase in leaf green and leave to dry. Peel off the mask and paint a flower in the masked-out area. Leave to dry, then decorate the edge of the oval with a lacy tracery of black outliner.

Grey Egyptian vase
Sponge all over this angled vase with a subtle grey colour. Leave to dry, then stencil the lotus flowers with white water-based paint, using a stencil brush.

Tall mosaic vase
Add a subtle decoration to this blue vase by creating square mosaic shapes quickly and easily with the tip of a flat brush. Begin at the top, working your way down, and add a row of contrasting colour for added variation.

Spun stripes vase
This straight-sided vase is the perfect shape to try out the spinning cake icing turntable method. Use diluted water-based paint on a large round brush to make the colour flow evenly. When the paint is dry, add a border of angled brush strokes.

Leaf Design Jug

A simple leaf motif, repeated in neat diagonal lines, forms a striking interlocking pattern to cover a jug or vase. The first line of leaves is painted between two guidelines and the rest of the motifs fit around this to keep the pattern even. The cool, spring green is ideal for decorating a flower jug, but blue paint on white china, using a similar motif, would make an elegant breakfast set.

You will need

peridot green

White china jug
Chinagraph pencil
Ruler
Masking tape
Small round watercolour brush
Water-based ceramic paints, such as Porcelaine 150, as shown above
Methylated spirits
Kitchen towel

1 Using the chinagraph pencil and ruler, draw two parallel lines on the jug about 1 cm (⅜ in) apart. The lines should run diagonally across the front of the jug. If you find it difficult to keep the ruler in place, tape one end of it to the jug with masking tape and hold the other end in position with your thumb.

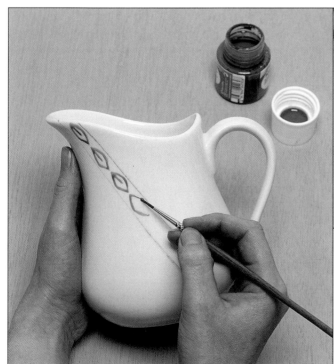

2 Using the small watercolour brush, paint a small leaf with a central vein at the top of the jug. Make sure the first leaf fits between the lines and then paint another just below it. Continue in this way to the bottom edge of the jug.

painting ceramics/project 10

3 Leave the first row of leaves until the paint is touch-dry, then wipe away one of the guidelines with a little methylated spirits on some kitchen paper.

4 Paint the second row of leaves close to the first. Interlock the shapes to keep the pattern even and the size of the leaves uniform. Work around the jug in this way until you get to where you started. Wipe away the other chinagraph pencil line before you complete the last row of leaves.

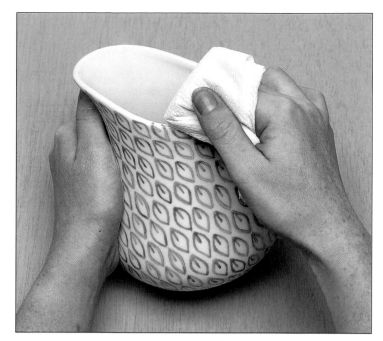 

5 To keep the edge of the jug clean without altering the pattern, paint the whole leaf over the edge and remove it later. To do this easily, wrap some damp kitchen paper around your fingertip and carefully run your finger along the edge of the jug to wipe off the paint cleanly.

6 When the painted leaves on the body of the jug are dry, you can work on the handle. For this, simply paint a single line of complete leaves down the length of the handle. Leave to dry for 24 hours, then bake the jug in the oven following the manufacturer's instructions.

Alternative design:

Blue leaves

Blue leaves, painted in a similar way across plates and mugs, will make a striking set. If you use a chinagraph pen to draw lines on the plate to keep the design regular, take care not to paint over these lines, as the water-based ceramic paint will not adhere to the waxy surface.

painting ceramics/project 10

11 PROJECT Pansy Pasta Bowls

Serve your pasta recipes in style from these colourful floral bowls. The freehand design, which was inspired by a curtain fabric, is drawn and masked out before the background colour is painted. The pansies, which float above the striking yellow background, are painted by hand using a range of blues and purples. Each flower looks slightly different, which gives the whole design a more naturalistic feel.

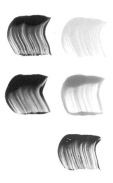

You will need

citrine

malachite

Ming blue

lapis

Parma violet

ivory white

White china serving bowl and dishes

Chinagraph pencil

Masking fluid

Medium-sized watercolour brush

Water-based ceramic paints, such as Porcelaine 150, as shown above

Palette

Fan-shaped brush

Kitchen towel

Small watercolour brushes

1 Using a chinagraph pencil, mark the edge of the bowls to divide them into seven equal sections. Using these marks to keep the spacing even, draw out the outlines of the pansies as shown. If you wish to draw the pansies first and then trace them, you can use the pencil transfer method as described on page 17 of the techniques chapter.

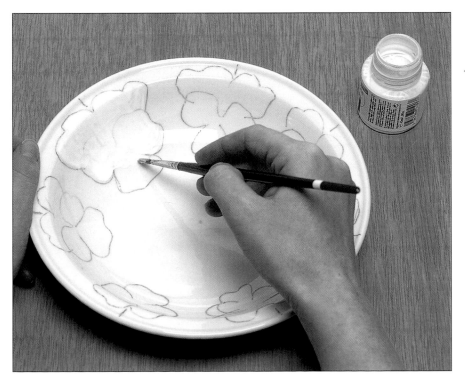

2 Using masking fluid and a medium-sized brush, paint all over the flower shapes, going right over the chinagraph lines. Leave this to dry completely.

3 Draw a slightly larger pansy in the centre of the bowl and paint over this with masking fluid. Rub off the dividing lines on the edge of the dish and paint the background shade – made by mixing citrine and malachite together – using the fan-shaped brush. Brush this colour onto the plate fairly sparingly in one direction. Don't try to aim for a smooth colour as the natural brush strokes will add to the design.

4 Leave this paint to dry hard for 24 hours, then rub off the film of dried masking fluid from each flower. Also rub off any remnants of chinagraph around the edges with a dry piece of kitchen towel.

5 Pour out the blues, purple and white paints onto a palette and use the medium-sized watercolour brush to paint the flowers. Start by mixing a pale mauve and paint over most of the petals, leaving a rough star shape in the centre of each flower.

artist's tip

Always wash out your brush at five minute intervals when using masking fluid, to avoid spoiling the brush by allowing the rubbery solution to dry in the bristles. The solution is water-soluble when it is wet, but not when it dries.

6 Mix the purple and blue paints and shade from the edge of the central area of the flower out towards the edges of the petals. Leave until touch-dry.

7 Paint the central star shape of each flower in yellow and leave to dry.

Paint each flower slightly differently for a more interesting look.

8 To complete each flower, paint a small cross in dark green at the centre. Leave the bowls to dry for 24 hours, then bake them in the oven following the manufacturer's instructions.

Alternative design:

Anemone bowls

You could use the same technique, using masking fluid, to paint different flowers. This bowl has been decorated with wild anemones in different colours, against a background covered with green felt tip swirls.

Serving Dishes
Gallery

Top shelf, left to right:

Continental pizza plate

This large, flat plate is decorated with a hand-painted design typical of continental-style china. The blue bands and central spiral are painted with diluted water-based ceramic paint applied with a large brush. To make these even, circular stripes, anchor the plate to a cake icing turntable with kneadable adhesive and spin it around whilst applying the paint. Leave to dry, then paint the leaves and lemons using a round brush and make the dotted patterns using cotton buds. To give the lemon its characteristic texture and to shade it slightly, a second coat of yellow paint has been applied using a cotton bud.

Zig-zag dish

Begin decorating this dish by sponging its flat outer edge with a natural sponge and water-based ceramic paint. Wipe off the excess with a damp cloth to clean the edges and leave to dry. Use a round brush to paint the stripes and zig-zag patterns diagonally across the centre of the dish. Leave to dry, then embellish the design with contrasting dots, outlines and wiggles using felt pens for china.

Square serving dish

This deep dish has a useful flat edge on which to paint this easy, modern design. Paint the corners using water-based ceramic paints and a large flat brush. Work from the inner edge to the outer edge of the dish with straight strokes and wipe off any excess paint with a damp cloth. Use the same brush to paint a series of wide stripes in red and yellow and two rows of blue squares on each side. Leave to dry, then use felt pens for china to draw straight, wiggly and dotted lines to complete the design.

Lower shelf, left to right :

Doily design cake stand

The decoration on this dish has been achieved by using a doily as a stencil. Cut a piece from a doily to fit the centre of your dish and apply spray adhesive to hold it in place. Use a stencil brush to dab the water-based paint through the holes in the doily, then lift off carefully. Leave to dry. Paint the pattern of leaf shapes round the edge following the picture and using a small round brush.

Classic blue and white oval dish

Use the shape of a dish like this to help your design. Start by masking the inner edge with flexible masking tape. Then sponge the dish with diluted blue water-based paint. Peel off the masking tape and clean up the edges with a damp cloth, then leave to dry. Using a brush, stencil a floral design in the centre using the same but undiluted colour and add hand-painted petal shapes around the edge.

Spotted blue and white vegetable dish

Quickly sponge all over the inside of the dish with blue water-based paint. While the paint is still wet, twist a clean cotton bud in the centre of the dish to remove a circle of paint. Repeat this around the first spot and continue in this way, changing the cotton buds frequently to maintain evenly sized spots. Clean up the edge of the sponged area with a damp cloth and finish off by painting a simple design around the edge.

Delicate hand-painted spice plant designs are the perfect decoration for these air-tight china jars. The varied selection of plants, including nutmeg, caraway and all-spice, with their intricate stems and leaves, are ideal for practising fine painting skills. Try drawing your own spice designs to add other spice plants, such as coriander, chilli and cardamom, to your collection.

You will need

olivine

peridot

emerald

malachite

amber

etruscan red

Small white china storage jars

Tracing paper

Hard and soft pencils

Masking tape

Water-based ceramic paints, such as Porcelaine 150, as shown above

Medium-sized watercolour brush

Long-haired watercolour brush

Palette

Tiny watercolour brush

Small watercolour brush

Cocktail stick

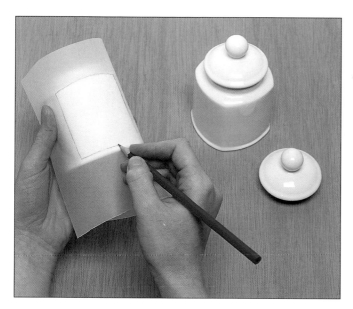

1 Wrap a piece of tracing paper around your spice jar and draw the outline of the area you wish to decorate. Trace one of the designs from page 94 into the centre of this area on the tracing paper. You can enlarge or reduce the designs using a photocopier to fit different sized jars.

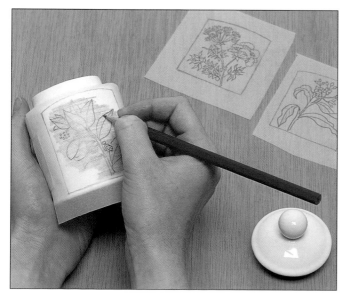

2 Clean the china thoroughly prior to painting or tracing. Scribble on the reverse of the traced design with the soft pencil, turn the paper around and tape it onto the jar with masking tape. Transfer the design to the surface of the china by going over the outline with a hard sharp pencil.

3 To make the nutmeg design, remove the tracing and use the olivine paint to paint the base coat of the leaves. Use the medium-sized brush making the brush strokes follow the length of each leaf.

4 When you have painted the leaves, use the long-haired brush to paint the stems and other flowing tendrils. It will hold enough paint to complete a whole stem in one stroke whilst still making a narrow line.

5 Leave the paint until touch-dry, then mix some of the other greens together on the palette and use this colour to shade the leaves. Paint darker green veins on the leaves using the tiny watercolour brush.

6 Mix the amber and etruscan red on the palette and paint the seeds and the nutmeg on the design using the small watercolour brush. Vary the colour slightly to shade the nutmeg shape. Paint the other designs on separate jars following the designs as shown on page 94 and the colours as shown on page 74.

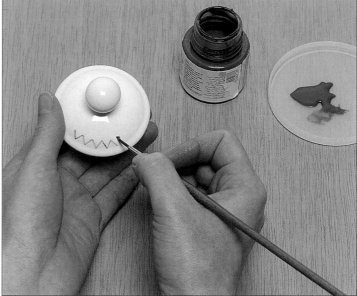

7   Decorate the top edge of each jar with a regular line of brush strokes. Use the medium-sized watercolour brush dipped into the the olivine paint and simply dab it flat onto the surface. Create a radiating pattern all round the edge of the jar.

8   Use the tiny brush to make a delicate zigzag line around the edge of each lid. Use the olivine paint again so that the colour matches the designs on the main part of the jar.

9   To complete the lid, make regular tiny dots quickly and easily around the lid using a cocktail stick. Dip the point directly into the paint and touch it lightly on to the china to form a tiny dot. Leave the jars to dry for 24 hours, then bake them in the oven following the manufacturer's instructions.

painting ceramics/project 12

This Zen sushi set made of fine white porcelain, complete with serving plates, napkin ring and dipping dish, is perfect for serving sushi and other oriental delicacies. The bold black pattern with an orange sun is reminiscent of Japanese designs and is simple to recreate by painting with fine brushes and a steady hand.

You will need

black

saffron

coral

Plain white rectangular plates, napkin rings and dipping dishes

Tracing paper

Soft pencil

Masking tape

Small coin

Water-based ceramic paints, such as Porcelaine 150, as shown above

Small, round watercolour brush

Medium-sized round watercolour brush

1 Carefully trace the larger oriental design on page 94 using the soft pencil. Check that the complete design will fit onto your plate and adjust if necessary. You can use a photocopier to enlarge or reduce the design if necessary.

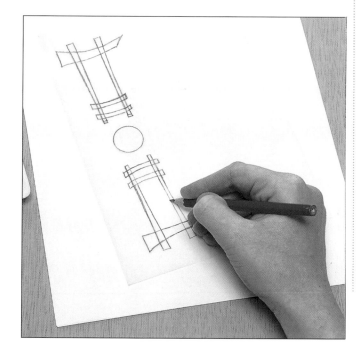

2 Turn over the tracing paper and tape the design in position on the plate. Now use a small coin to rub over the back of the design to transfer it to the plate. Meticulously go over each line.

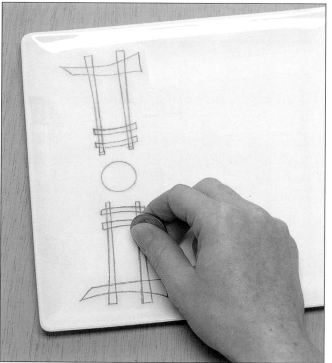

3 Remove the tape from one side and lift the tracing paper to check that the design is being transferred correctly. If the design has transferred to the plate clearly, remove the tracing paper. If not, replace the tracing paper and continue rubbing with the coin.

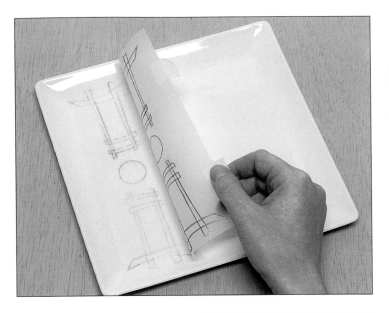

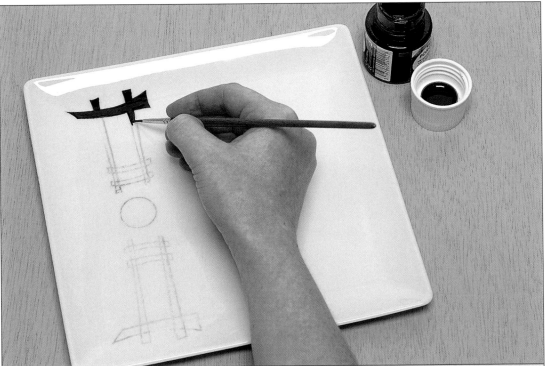

4 Use the small watercolour brush to paint the main shape in black, taking care not to smudge the pencil lines as you work. Do not apply too much paint to start with, as you can always add more to make a dense black once the first coat has dried. Paint both motifs in this way.

artist's tip

Use a damp cloth to wipe off the pencil marks after you have fired the china to avoid damaging the painting.

5 In a clean palette, mix some of the coral and saffron paints together to make a deep orange for the sun. Use the small brush to carefully paint the outline of the sun in between the black motifs.

6 Change to a medium-sized watercolour brush to fill in the centre of the sun, floating the paint over the surface to make an even coating.

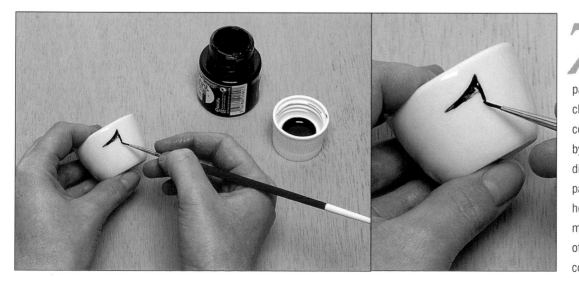

7 Use the small watercolour brush to paint the small oriental character from page 94 freehand onto the smaller china pieces. If you make a mistake, correct it while the paint is still wet by wiping it off with a cotton bud dipped in water. Leave all the painted pieces to dry for at least 24 hours, then bake them following the manufacturer's instructions. Turn off the heat and leave the pieces to cool before use.

Vivid colours and strong outlines are the hallmark of Art Deco designs, such as those created by Clarice Cliff. This teaset pays homage to the Art Deco style with a typical cottage scene, outlined in black and then painted in bold, primary colours. The watercolour ceramic paints give true glossy colours and the latest felt pens for ceramics will make the outlines look really professional.

You will need

scarlet

saffron

Marseille yellow

peridot

calcite

lapis

black felt pen

White china teaset

Tracing paper

Hard and soft pencils

Masking tape

Water-based ceramic paints, such as Porcelaine 150 paints, as shown above

Medium-sized watercolour brush

Small watercolour brush

Felt pen as shown above

1 Clean the whole teaset thoroughly before you start working. Trace the two designs from page 94 ready to transfer to the china. These designs can be enlarged or reduced on a photocopier to enable them to fit most pieces of china. You could also continue the lines and add extra trees or bushes to extend the design. After you have traced the design on one side, scribble on the reverse with the soft pencil.

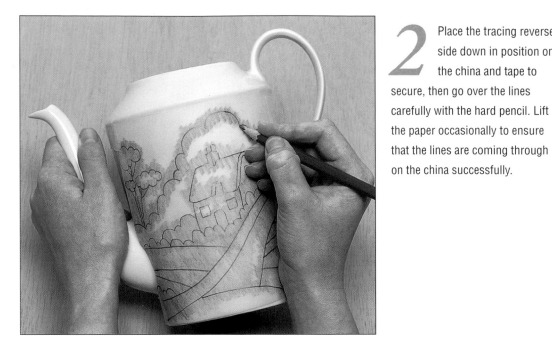

Place the tracing reverse side down in position on the china and tape to secure, then go over the lines carefully with the hard pencil. Lift the paper occasionally to ensure that the lines are coming through on the china successfully.

3 When you have completed the design, lift off the tracing carefully and take care not to smudge the lines as you work. Transfer the design just before painting each item, as the pencil lines will rub off quite easily.

4 Using the medium-sized brush, paint in some of the larger areas following the colours as shown on the finished set. Try to paint in a smooth coat without excessive brush marks. You may find that some colours will need a second coat to achieve the right depth of colour, but leave the first coat until it is touch-dry before applying the second.

5 Use the small watercolour brush to apply paint to the smaller areas and those with more complex shapes, painting right up to the outlines. Leave the paint until touch-dry before painting the adjacent area, so that the colours don't run into each other.

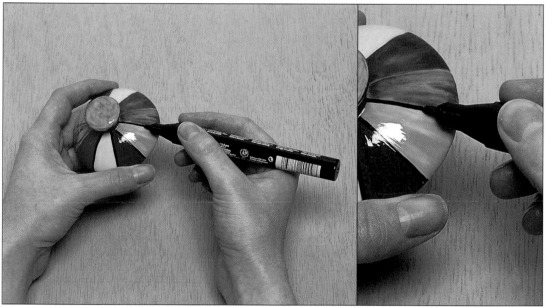

6 Paint the teapot lid with contrasting bands of colours and leave the paint to dry. Leave all of the painted items to dry overnight so that the paint will harden. Use the black felt pen to draw in the outlines around each shape and between every colour. Leave for 24 hours, then bake in the oven following the manufacturer's instructions.

The smaller design is perfect for cups and a milk jug. The felt pen will make beautifully even lines around each colour, and you can also fill in small areas successfully.

Add a few freehand, criss-cross lines using the black felt pen on the bridge area to indicate brickwork.

When you have mastered a variety of china painting techniques – using a range of brushes – try your hand at this artistic vase following the style of the French Impressionists. You don't need to follow a rigid design as it is simply a random mix of fields, woodland and hedgerows below a swirling, cloudy sky. Keep the brush strokes free and vigorous for a lively Impressionist style.

You will need

opaline blue

opaline green

white

red

turquoise

Ming blue

calcite

peridot

malachite

green felt pen

White pottery or china vase

Water-based ceramic paints, such as Porcelaine 150, as shown above

Palette

Fan-shaped brush

Medium-sized round watercolour brush

Small flat watercolour brush

Felt pen as shown above

Small round watercolour brush

1 Clean the vase thoroughly. A postcard or print of a favourite painting can act as reference for the paint technique. Pour a little of the opaline blue paint onto a palette, then, using the fan-shaped brush, spread the paint fairly thinly over the top third of the vase. Paint the sky area all around the vase allowing the brush strokes to flow horizontally.

2 Repeat this process with the opaline green paint to cover the lower part of the vase. Blend the colours softly together at the horizon to avoid a hard, straight line. Leave this to dry for 24 hours before painting the details on top.

3 Using the medium-sized watercolour brush, paint the top of the clouds with the white paint. Build up the shape of the clouds using short brush strokes. To add definition to the clouds, shade the lower areas with a mix of the blue, white and grey paints working down as far as the horizon.

4 To complete the sky, use the small flat brush to make short strokes in a mix of blue and turquoise. Allow some of the background colour to show through the brush strokes for a lively texture.

5 Use the green felt pen to draw the outlines of the fields. Make very light dotted guidelines and also draw in tiny trees and hedgerows. When the felt pen outlines have dried, use the small round brush to paint the fields in various natural colours of greens, white and ochre. Mix your colours on a palette to make a varied selection of subtle shades.

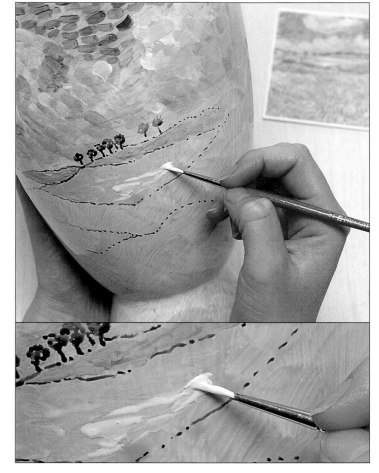

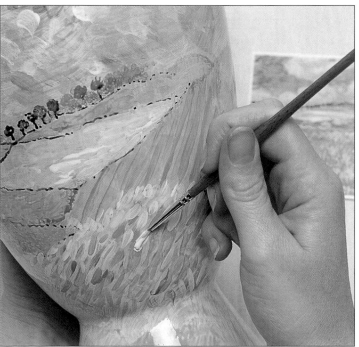

artist's tip

For a quick and easy way to make furrows and parallel lines in your painted fields, use a cocktail stick or wooden skewer, drawn lightly through the wet paint to reveal the base colour.

6 For the foreground, paint the long grass with angled brush strokes in shades of green, white and ochre using the small round brush. Continue this down to the base of the vase and leave until it is touch-dry, then add a few thin lines with the green felt pen to define individual blades of grass. To finish the composition, paint small, random spots of red to represent poppies in the fields in the foreground. Leave the vase to dry for at least 24 hours, then bake it in the oven following the manufacturer's instructions.

Junk Shop Finds
Gallery

Top shelf, left to right:

Purple passion
(Artist: Judy Balchin)
This beautifully shaped teapot has been roughly painted with a mix of blue and red. Leave to dry, then use gold outliner to add tiny "V" shapes all over, and a gold edge and knob.

Greek key design
This sturdy 1950s teapot needs a strong design. The stencilled black key design was embellished with gold outliner.

Black and gold candlestick
This free scribble design is ideal for practising the use of gold outliner. The plain candlestick gains much in character with this gold texture.

Victorian candlestick
This pretty white candlestick is typical of Victorian dressing table sets. The addition of painted pink and mauve flowers and stripes gives it even more character.

See the light
To blend a plain table lamp into your colour scheme, paint the base following the moulding of the china. Before you fire it in the oven, you need to remove any plastic fitments and leads which would melt in the heat.

Middle shelf, left to right:

Tea for one
(Artist: Judy Balchin)
This cup, saucer and teapot set makes the perfect morning cup of tea with colours guaranteed to wake you up.

Art Deco tile
(Artist: Judy Balchin)
Paint this charming scene onto a tile purely for decoration. Draw the design in outliner first and leave to dry. Then flood each area with colour to give a rich stained glass look.

Stars and spirals tile
Another tile design which would contrast well with plain tiles can be achieved with a star stamp. When the stars are dry, add spirals using green and turquoise felt pens for china.

Striped dish
Use a wide flat brush to make even stripes down the side of a useful dish. You could use this simple idea to add extra serving dishes to an existing dinner set by painting the stripes in co-ordinating colours.

Flower power
(Artist: Judy Balchin)
Stylized flowers can be painted with single brush strokes forming the petals, stems and leaves for a quick and easy design. Add a coloured edge to complete.

Lower shelf, left to right:

Italian look cup and saucer
(Artist: Judy Balchin)
The bold and colourful shapes are painted with single brush strokes to give this sturdy china a continental look.

Violets cup and saucer
Tiny flowers, painted in a realistic style using a fine brush, make a pretty design. Start with one cup and saucer and you could end up painting a whole tea set.

Retro cup and saucer
Quickly splash random swirls of red, orange and turquoise all over the china, then leave to dry. Complete the design with bold spirals of black outliner.

Bold brushwork dish (Artist: Duncan Green)
Reminiscent of modern Japanese designs, this square sushi dish has been decorated with strong brush strokes in rich blue and lilac.

Tea leaf pot
No need to plan this design first: simply start painting a small branch of leaves and buds and soon you'll find the design is growing over the whole pot.

Templates

The templates on these pages are actual size
unless enlargement to 200% is indicated.

Safari Teapot and Mugs
(page 36)

Mexican Wave Tiles
(page 42, enlarge to 200%)

Topiary Tree Plant Pots
(page 32)

Shell Design Bathroom Set

(page 52)

Nutmeg

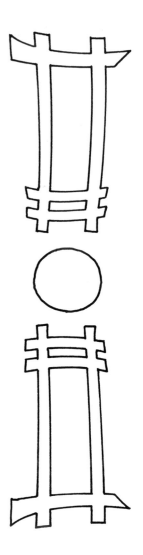

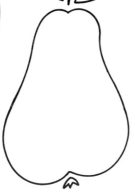

Stencilled Fruit Plates

(page 58, enlarge to 200%)

Caraway

All-spice

Spice Storage Jars

(page 74)

Zen Sushi Set

(page 78)

Art Deco Teaset

(page 82, enlarge to 200%)

Suppliers

UK

Fred Aldous
PO Box 135
37 Lever Street
Manchester M1 1LW
Tel: (0161) 236 2477
Fax: (0161) 236 6075
(Mail order suppliers of china
paints, brushes and many craft
products)

Panduro Hobby
Westway House
Transport Avenue
Brentford
Middx TW8 9HF
Tel: (020) 8847 6161
(Mail order suppliers of china
paints, brushes and a wide
range of craft products)

Pébéo UK Ltd
109 Solent Business Centre
Milbrook Road West, Milbrook
Southampton SO15 0HW
Tel: (0170) 390 1914
Fax: (0170) 390 1906
Website: www.pebeo.com
(Supplier of all Pébéo paints in
this country; ring for your
nearest stockist)

Philip and Tacey Ltd
North Way, Andover
Hampshire SP10 5BA
Tel: (01264) 332171
(Suppliers of Pébéo Porcelaine
150 paints, china items to
paint, and many craft items for
use in china painting. Ring for
your nearest stockist)

Specialist Crafts Ltd
Unit 2, Wanlip Road Ind Est
Syston, Leicester LE7 1PA
Tel: (0116) 269 7711
(Mail order supplier of china
paints, brushes and a wide
range of craft products)

F Trauffler Ltd
100 East Road
London N1 6AA
Tel: (020) 7251 0240
Fax: (020) 7251 0242
(Supplier of plain white china
by Apilco)

SOUTH AFRICA

Art Mates
Musgrave Centre
124 Musgrave Road
Durban
Tel: (031) 21-0094

Bowker Arts and Crafts
52 4th Avenue
Newton Park
Port Elizabeth
Tel: (041) 35-2487

The Craftsman
Progress House
110 Bordeaux Drive
Randburg
Johannesburg
Tel: (011) 787-1846

Crafty Supplies
The Atrium
32 Main Road
Claremont
Cape Town
Tel: (021) 61-0308

Le Papier du Port
Gardens Centre
Cape Town
Tel: (021) 462-4796
Mail order service:
PO Box 50055
Waterfront 8002

Liserfam Invest. (Pty) Ltd
PO Box 1721
Bedfordview 2008
Johannesburg
Tel: (011) 455-6810

Schweikerdts (Pty) Ltd
475 Fehrsen Street
Pretoria
Tel: (012) 46-5406
Mail order service:
PO Box 697
Pretoria 0001

AUSTRALIA

Brookvale Hobby Ceramics
9 Powelles Road
Brookvale NSW 2100
Tel: (02) 9905 0264

Ceramic and Craft Centre
52 Wecker Road
Mansfield 3722
Queensland
Tel: (07) 3343 7377
Fax: (07) 3349 5052
Branches throughout Australia

Ceramic Hobbies Pty Ltd
12 Hanrahan Street
Thomastown 3074
Victoria
Tel: (03) 466 2522
Fax: (03) 9464 0547

The Craft House
51-55 Seymour Street
Ringwood VIC
Tel: (03) 9870 4522
Fax: (03) 9870 4788

Elliot, Fay & Paul Good
31 Landsdown Terrace
Walkerville SA 5081
Tel: (08) 8344 4306

Francheville
1-5 Perry Street
Collingwood
VIC 3066
Tel: (03) 9416 0611
Fax: (03) 9416 0584
Suppliers of Pébéo paints
including Porcelaine 150 and
Deco.
Telephone for your nearest
stockist.
Please also contact for
New Zealand stockists.

Mals Hobby Ceramics
3093 Albany Highway
Armadale WA 6065
Tel: (08) 9399 7746

NEW ZEALAND

Auckland Folk Art Centre
591 Remuera Road
Upland Village
Auckland
Tel: (09) 524 0936

Dominion Paint Centre
227 Dominion Road
Mt Eden
Tel: (0800) 555 959

Draw Art Supplies Ltd
5 Mahunga Drive
Mangere Bridge
Tel: (09) 636 4862

P A Inkham Ltd
(Rubber Stamp
Manufacturers)
43 Mt Eden Road
Eden Terrace
Auckland
Tel: (09) 367 1085

Paint The Earth
475 Lake Road
Takapuna
Tel: (09) 489 1117

QT Ceramics and Crafts
H/18 Tamariki Ave
Orewa
Tel: (09) 4267478

Studio Art Supplies
81 Parnell Rise
Parnell
Auckland
Tel: (09) 377 0302

Index